GW01217878

Shollie
20 Milestone Challenges

Shollie Memorable Moments. Includes Milestones for
Memories, Gifts, Grooming, Socialization & Training

Volume 2

Todays Doggy

Copyright © 2019

Dedicated To All of You Wonderful Owners and Fans

Introduction

Welcome to the Original Doggy Milestone Series™ where you are encouraged to create those special moments with your dog. We have composed the milestones in a way that challenges you to set the stage before taking your photos.

Use props and make it fun - be creative in setting up your photos. Get family and friends involved - take it out with you - use it in different places and settings - have a play with it and most importantly, have a good time!

You can either hold the desired milestone spread open yourself - or have somebody hold it open as you take the snap.

If you would like to have the selected milestone book spread open and standing independently in your photos, you can use one or two large 'foldback' clips to hold the spread open.

Share your photos with friends, family, and communities - look for feedback and areas of improvements in order to create even better memorable photos.

Good luck and enjoy your photo fun.

I
Noticed
You
Were
Sleeping...

So I Helped You Finish The Food

I Look Rather Fetching

...Don't I ?

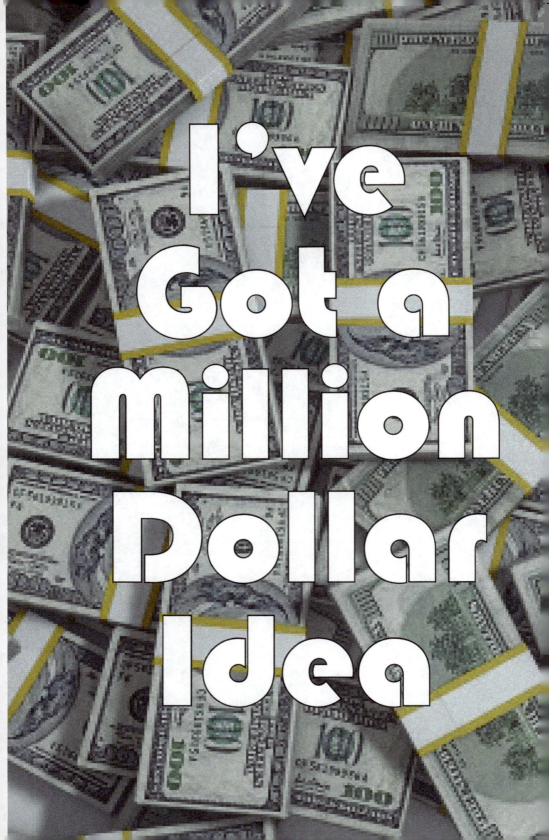

SORRY...

Too Busy To Talk!

...Bad
To The
Bone

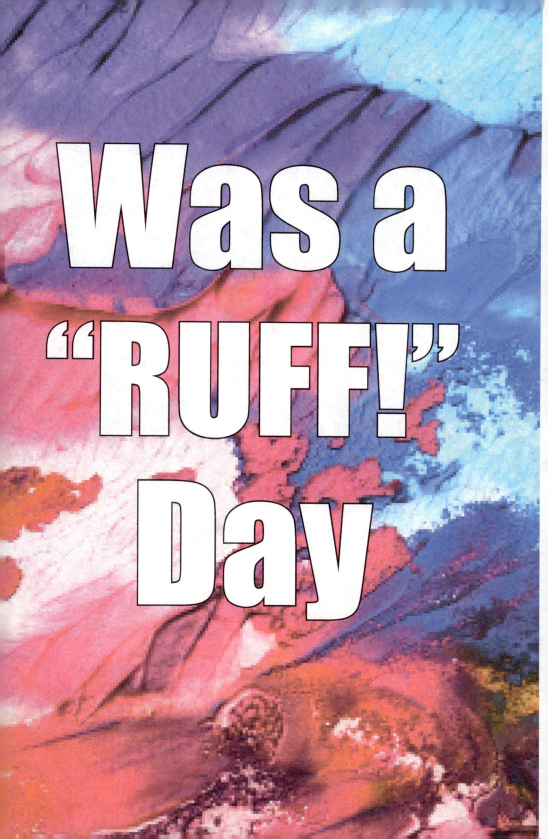

I Have No Idea

What I'm Doing

WHEN YOU'RE HOME ALONE

AND
SOMEONE KNOCKS ON THE DOOR...

MIRROR MIRROR ON THE WALL...

Who's The Doggiest Of Them All?

I'm So GREAT

I Even Know How To High 5

The Joys of Being Groomed

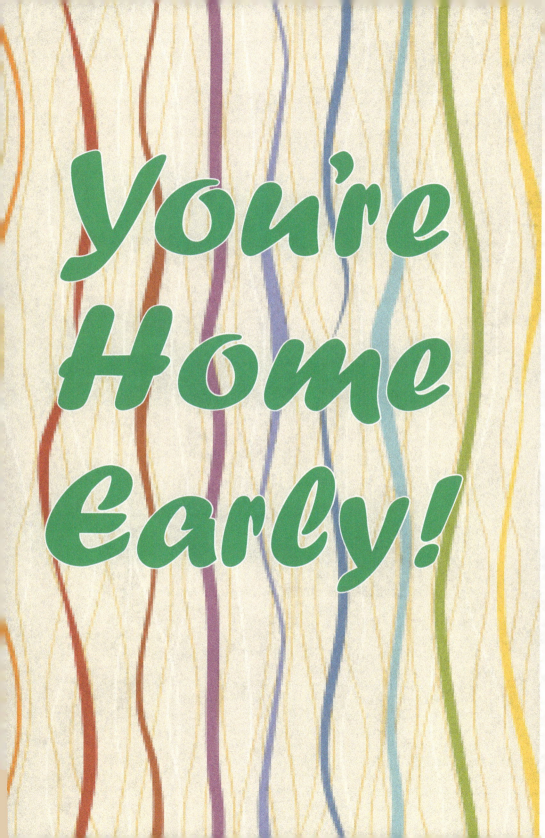

I'm Not Lazy

I'm Just On Energy Saving Mode

OH LOOK!

Someone Has Made a Mess!

I
Wonder
Who
Did It!?

As You Can See

I'm
Sleeping

Your Secrets Are Safe With Me

I'm
Always
Listening

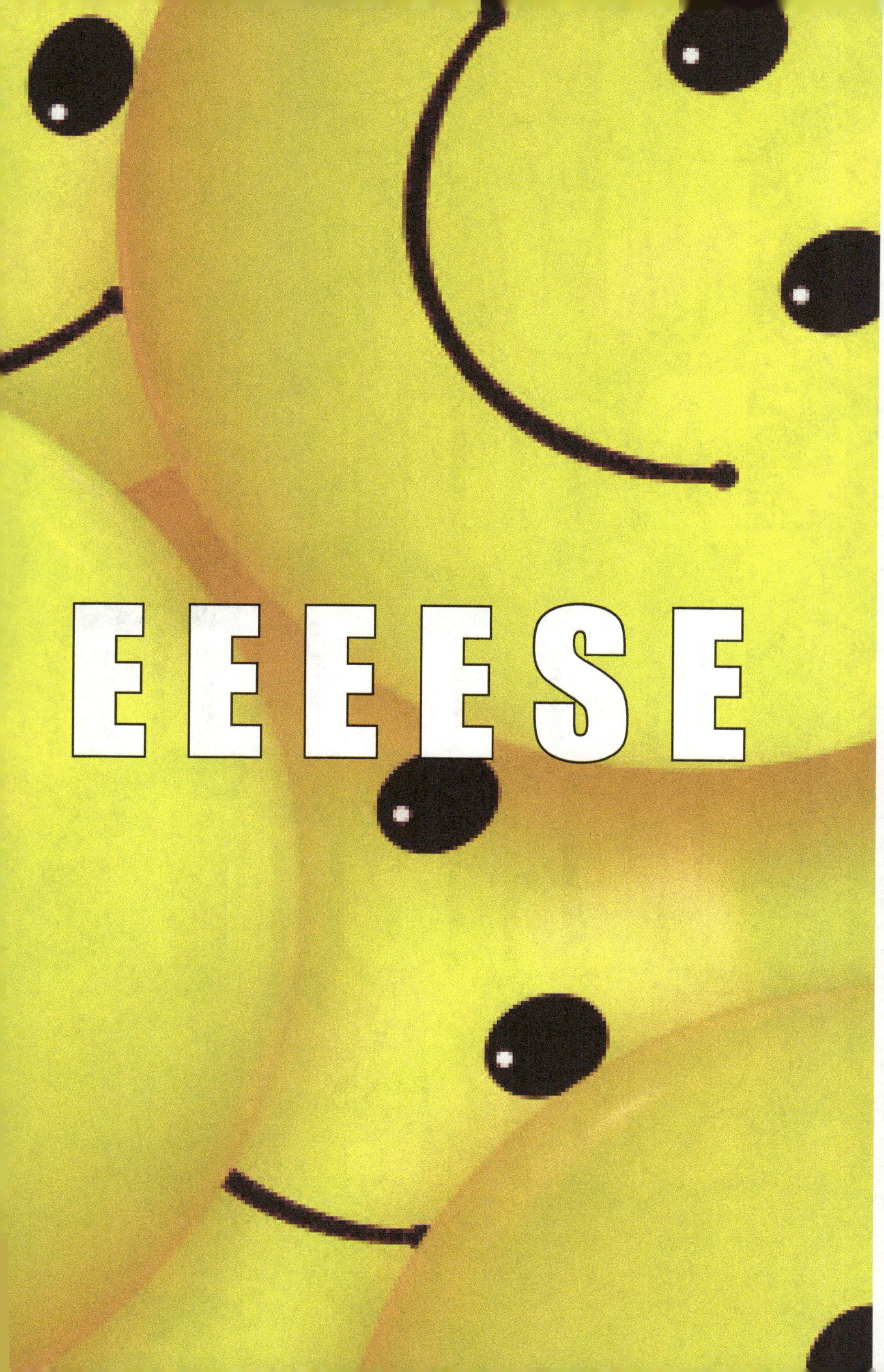
EEESE

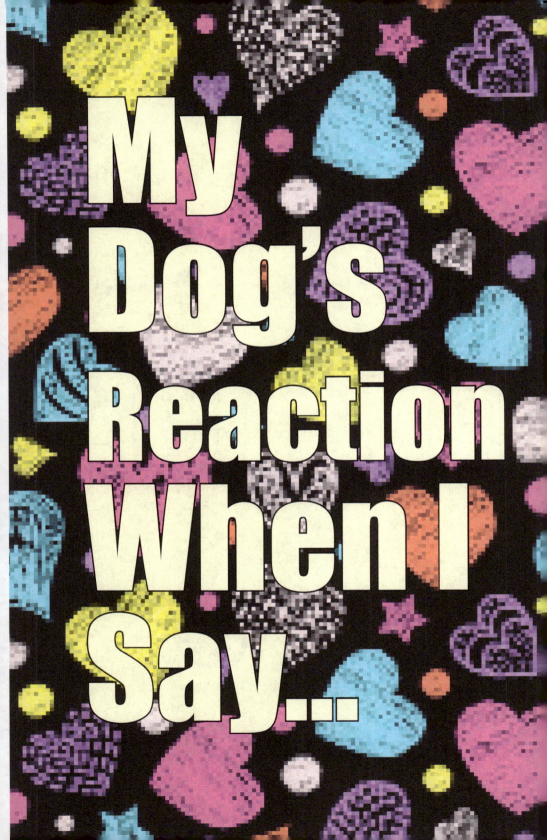

My Dog's Reaction When I Say...

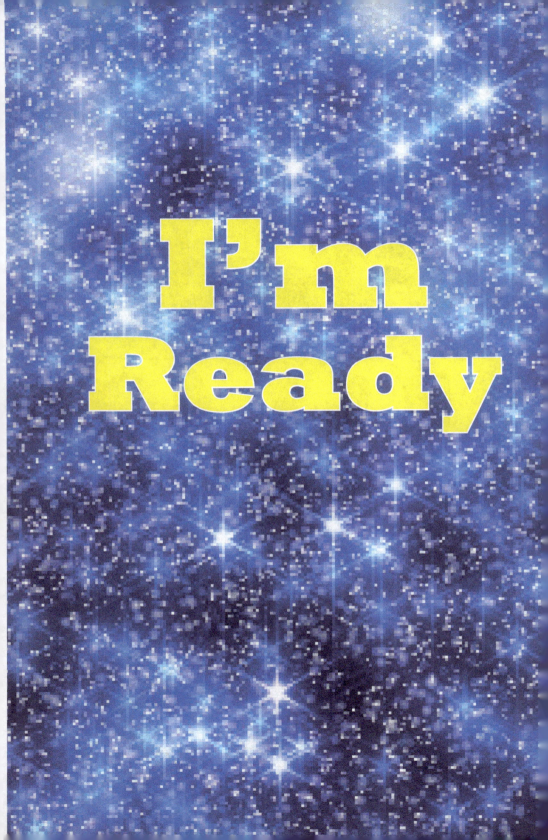

For My

Bedtime Story

I've Got It All...

Under
Control

CPSIA information can be obtained
at www.ICGtesting.com
Printed in the USA
BVHW060208140919
558390BV00008B/743/P

9 781395 348670